THE LITTLE GREEN AVOCADO BOOK

Linda Doeser

PIATKUS

Other titles in the series

The Little Garlic Book
The Little Pepper Book
The Little Lemon Book
The Little Apple Book
The Little Strawberry Book

© 1981 Judy Piatkus (Publishers) Limited

First published in 1981 by Judy Piatkus
(Publishers) Limited of Loughton, Essex

Reprinted 1982
Reprinted 1983
Reprinted 1984
Reprinted 1987

British Library Cataloguing in Publication Data

Doeser, Linda
    The little green avocado book.
    1. Avocado
    I. Title
    634′.653   SB379.A9
    ISBN 0-86188-125-7

Drawings by Linda Broad

Designed by Ken Leeder

Cover photograph by courtesy of Carmel Produce of Israel

Typeset by The Blackmore Press, Shaftesbury
Printed and bound at The Bath Press, Avon

CONTENTS

THE AVOCADO PEAR TREE

The delicious avocado, with its delicate, almost nut-like flavour, is the fruit of the avocado pear tree, a member of the laurel family, Lauraceae. The species is called *Persea americana* or *Persea gratissima* and it is one of about 2,000 different species of trees and shrubs that make up the laurel family. They are mainly tropical and evergreen and include cinnamon, sassafras, camphor and sweet bay, or poet's laurel.

Avocado pear trees can be either short, spreading and fairly bushy or grow erect to a height of 60 feet or more. Usually the trunk is crooked and the branches low. The volatile oil in the thick, fleshy bark smells of aniseed. Crush the leaves of the Mexican avocado pear tree and they, too, will smell of it. The wood is rather soft and brittle and prone to wind damage.

The leaves are evergreen, leathery and elliptical, sometimes even egg-shaped, in form. A few varieties shed their leaves when the tree flowers but new foliage quickly appears. This has a reddish tinge but soon turns bright green.

Small and inconspicuous greenish or yellow flowers are crowded on the ends of branches. It can take 5,000 of these petal-less flowers to produce one mature fruit—and a tree can produce between 100 and 500 avocados in a season. The flowers are bisexual, fragrant and pollinated by bees, but the species has a remarkable way of preventing self-pollination. There are two types of cultivated varieties. In one type, the flowers open in the morning and the female part is receptive. They then close. In the afternoon they re-open and this time the pollen is ripe. In the other type, the cycle is reversed. Naturally, commercial growers interplant the two.

The fruit is not a pear at all, but a berry. To confuse matters further, it contains so much oil and protein that it could almost be classified as a vegetable. The 'pears' grow in clusters of three to five and, as there are about 400 commercial varieties, there is quite a large range of sizes, shapes and colours. Some avocados are no bigger than a plum, others grow to a phenomenal size and can weigh as much as 4 pounds. Shapes vary from the familiar pear-shape to almost spherical and the skin may be as thin as that of a dessert apple or thick, coarse and woody in texture. Colours range through green, sometimes tinged with crimson, to very dark purple. The flesh of the ripe fruit is invariably soft and buttery in consistency and yellowish or green in colour. Different varieties ripen at different times of the year.

The fruit is picked at weekly intervals when it is mature but not yet ripe. Ripe avocados perish very quickly. The branches are too brittle to support ladders and long picking poles with cloth bags on the ends have to be used. In larger orchards, harvesting is carried out with the aid of truck-mounted platforms.

Each pear has a single large seed. Trees are propagated from seed and by side grafting or shield budding. They are relatively easy to grow and require little attention apart from occasional pruning to encourage spreading, but both the flowers and the fruit are susceptible to frost damage. The roots are shallow and they cannot tolerate waterlogging or saline conditions. Good drainage is essential and in some places trees have to be grown on small mounds. In Central America, however, seedlings grow in the gardens and courtyards and thrive on practically no attention whatsoever.

The main disease is root rot and trees may be attacked by such things as thripe, scale, mealy bugs, red spider and weevil. But, by and large, they are pest- and disease-free. Fungi can attack the fruit in store, although proper care and ventilation will prevent this.

TYPES OF AVOCADOS

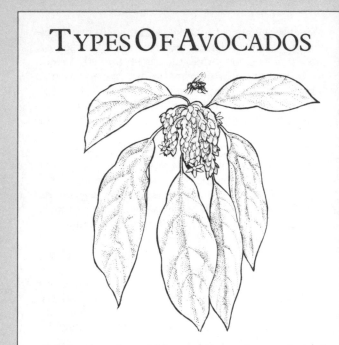

The avocados which we enjoy today are derived from three natural races—Mexican (semi-tropical), Guatemalan (subtropical) and West Indian (tropical).

The first type is native to the highlands of Mexico and is the hardiest of the three. The pears are small and weigh between 3 and 8 ounces. They have thin, smooth skins and the seeds are comparatively large and loose in the cavities. The flesh has a rich flavour and excellent quality. Its oil content may be as high as

30 per cent. The flowers are rather hairy and the leaves smell distinctly of aniseed—but this rarely pervades the fruit. Some botanists regard the Mexican avocado pear as a separate species and have given it the name *Persea drymifolia*. Cultivated varieties and hybrids are valuable commercially. They have been introduced to California, Chile and the Mediterranean and include Ettinger and Zutano.

The Guatemalan avocado is native to the highlands of Central America. It is less resistant to cold and the fruits are larger, weighing between 8 ounces and 2 pounds. The skins are thick, hard and brittle, often 'warty'. The pulp has an oil content of between 8 and 15 per cent. The seeds are small and held tightly by the flesh. Cultivated varieties include Hass, Taylor, Nabal and Lula.

The West Indian avocado is the most tropical in character and is native to the lowlands of Central America. Its leaves are lighter in colour and the fruits have smooth, leathery skins and are frequently very large, weighing between 2 and 3 pounds. The oil content is low, between 3 and 10 per cent, and the quality is excellent. The best known are Trapp and Pollock.

A third species of avocado pear tree grows in southern Mexico and Guatemala. It is called *Persea schiedeana* and it has only recently been introduced to the United States.

CULTIVATED VARIETIES

An acre of land will yield a larger amount of food when planted with avocados than it will when planted with any other tree crop. No wonder horticulturalists have taken such a keen interest this century in developing the fruit. Breeding programmes have been set up in California, Israel and elsewhere and superior seedlings have been selected within each race for clonal propagation. Breeders have concentrated on the suitability of seedlings to climate and soil conditions, heavy fruiting varieties, shipping quality, size and appearance and, of course, consumer satisfaction. Orchards have been established and self-pollination encouraged to maintain uniform fruit.

Surprisingly, despite these intensive efforts, the most successful varieties have been developed by individuals from chance seedlings and rarely has even the female parent been known.

There are now more than 400 cultivated varieties. The best known and commercially most important are Ettinger, Fuerte, Nabal and Hass.

The Ettinger avocado is medium to large and almost conical in shape. The skin is mid-green, thin and smooth. It is an important crop in Israel and is available from mid-autumn to mid-winter.

The Fuerte is a Mexican and Guatemalan hybrid. It is slightly smaller than the Ettinger, but still medium-sized. It is characteristically pear-shaped with a speckled, green skin and greenish flesh. It is resistant to cold and forms a major crop in California, Israel and South Africa.

The Nabal is about the same size or slightly smaller than the Fuerte but it is spherical in shape. The skin is dark green, tinged with crimson.

The Hass is the smallest of these four varieties and is easily recognised by its dark purple, knobbly skin. The flesh is pale yellow. It is in season from late-winter and throughout the spring and summer. Hass is becoming widely cultivated in the orchards of California and Israel.

GROWING REGIONS

T he avocado pear has been a major food in
Central America for thousands of years and it
has been said to be the most important single
contribution made by the New World to the human
diet. Today, it is one of the most popular of tropical
fruits and rivals bananas, pineapples and mangoes in
acreage and export.

The natural growing area extends from Mexico
south to the Columbian Andes. Seedlings were
introduced to other parts of the world from the
seventeenth century onwards and it now forms an
important commercial crop in Mexico, the West
Indies, Australia, South Africa, Israel and in Florida,
California and Texas in the United States. It is also
grown in commercial quantities in Hawaii, Chile,

Brazil, Madeira, the Philippines and in several Mediterranean countries. It is grown in other parts of Africa and in Asia, but only for domestic use.

SOME FACTS AND FIGURES

Every year, more and more people discover the avocado. Production is on the up and up. One tree can yield up to 500 avocados and some orchards produce over 5 tons of fruit per acre. Export is increasing and avocados are being shipped to markets all round the world. The figures below give some idea of the size of the operation.

The United States, in the season November 1978 to October 1979, produced 130,446 tons of avocados.

In November and December 1979 alone, the yield was an incredible 91,334 tons. In 1978/79, 7,735 tons were exported to more than 15 different countries, including Canada, the EEC, Hong Kong and Japan. During the 1978/79 season, 277 tons were exported to Britain. In 1979/80, that figure increased by almost 100 per cent—and it's still going up.

Mexico produced 373,000 tons in 1979, occupying a cultivated area of 111,197 acres (174 square miles). The main export markets for Mexican avocados are the United States, Canada, West Germany and France. Recently, Mexico has begun exporting to Britain.

South Africa, in 1979, exported 10,644 tons, about one-third of these to Britain. The main market is France, and some go to West Germany. Total production for the 1979/80 season was 19,962 tons.

In 1979, Israel produced 32,000 tons. Of these, 26,000 tons were exported, 70 per cent to France and 5 per cent to Britain. Israel can produce enough avocados to supply all the European markets.

Australia, in 1980, exported 1,442 tons of avocados, compared with 553 tons in 1979. In 1979/80, Queensland produced 941 tons from 42,000 trees.

AVOCADO HISTORY

There is strong evidence to suggest that avocado pear trees were flourishing 50 million years ago in what is now California. And it is not impossible that avocados were providing food for dinosaurs some 136 million years ago. Well-preserved fossils found in Cretaceous rocks indicate the existence of plants of the laurel family, similar to sassafras and Persea.

In tropical Central America the tree has been growing wild for thousands of years, providing a nutritious source of food, rich in oil and protein. The fruit partly replaces meat in native diets to this very day. Archaeologists have come across abundant remains of avocado seeds in Mexico which date back to 8000 BC, and in Peru, dating back to 2000 BC.

No-one knows exactly when enterprising farmers first began to cultivate the trees rather than simply harvesting the wild crops. Aztecs certainly took avocado seedlings from Ecuador to Mexico during the thirteenth, fourteenth and fifteenth centuries, and the Incas introduced the plant to Peru sometime between 1450 and 1475. When the Spanish conquistadors overran the Aztec and Incan empires in the early sixteenth century they found avocados under extensive home cultivation from Mexico south to Peru and as far east as Venezuela. The first written account of an avocado was made in 1526 by Gonzalo Hernandez de Oviedo and concerned a tree growing in Columbia, near the Isthmus of Panama.

The Aztecs called the tree *Ahuacatl* and the

victorious Spanish armies changed this to the similar sounding *abocado* or *avocado*, by which name it is now known throughout the English-speaking world. *Avocado* literally means advocate and the French adopted the same judicial name, calling the tree *avocat*. In modern Spanish-speaking countries, including Mexico, it is now called *aguacate*.

The Spaniards were the first Europeans to taste avocados but they were much more interested in pursuing the gold of the mythical El Dorado than in the commercial possibilities of tropical fruit. However, it was introduced to southern Spain in 1601 and to Jamaica in 1650. Sailors and soldiers from other European countries, lured to Central America and the West Indies by the promise of treasure, also became familiar with avocado pears, which must have provided a longed-for nutritious treat after a diet of weevil-ridden ship's biscuit.

At one time, the English called the avocado subaltern's butter and midshipman's butter. As these were inferior ranks, this suggests that the avocado was not held in great esteem. It was also known as poor man's butter, which suggests the same thing. However, these names probably resulted from the fact that the avocado was so abundant in Mexico and very rich in oil, whereas butter was a rare commodity, especially in a hot climate after a long voyage.

The word 'butter' is prominent among the popular names for the fruit. Butter pear was also commonly used in the seventeenth and eighteenth centuries. This clearly derived from the smooth and creamy texture of the flesh and its high oil content. The pale yellow colour of the flesh of some varieties may also have influenced this choice of names. Certainly, avocado pears could (and can) be spread on bread or biscuits just like butter.

It is also easy to see where the misnomer pear came from, for some varieties of avocados closely resemble pears in appearance and many have the characteristic shape. The popular name alligator pear dates from the seventeenth century and probably arose from the appearance of the dark, rough-textured Guatemalan avocado. Avocado producers now feel that this is a rather unattractive name and they are widely discouraging its use. In 1692, W. Hughes, writing in *The American Physician*, called it the Spanish pear and described it as 'one of the most rare and pleasant fruits, it nourisheth and strengtheneth the body.'

Wholesale import of avocados into Europe was not practical in the unpredictable and often hazardous days of sailing ships. Some fruit did find its way on to European tables and it has been known in England since the end of the seventeenth century. A few of the indomitable and pioneering horticulturalists of the past did attempt to grow avocado trees but the British climate proved too much for these tropical plants.

In the early 1900s, there was a sudden upsurge of interest in the avocado pear. Expeditions were made to Mexico and Guatemala and to other parts of Central America and northern South America. Grafting techniques and cultivation generally became more sophisticated and technically advanced. It became possible to establish commercial orchards with a reasonable guarantee of consistent quality and size of fruit. The trees had been introduced into California in 1848 and now cultivation began in earnest. Out of all the numerous seeds and budwood brought back to the United States, the Fuerte variety, found in the mountains of south Mexico, proved perfectly suited to the Californian climate and soil conditions. By the 1920s, the production of avocados had become a sizeable industry. Not long afterwards, the avocado was introduced to other American states and to countries as far away as Israel, South Africa and Australia.

For many years in Britain, the avocado pear remained a gourmet fruit, known and loved by the rich and well-travelled, who were used to dining in the world's best restaurants. By the late 1950s, it had begun to appear on less exalted dining tables and its aficionados were quick to spread the word of their new discovery. Now, increasingly huge quantities are imported every year and the avocado pear is seen in shops and supermarkets throughout the country.

Nutritional Values

The avocado pear is definitely something special. It is remarkably nutritious and contains 11 vitamins, 14 minerals and, for a fruit, plenty of protein. The carbohydrate content is low and it has no cholesterol. The flesh is rich in oil. In some varieties this can reach 30 per cent. Avocado oil is easy to digest and is very similar to olive oil, containing 75 per cent unsaturated fatty acids.

For those concerned about their waistlines, half an average-sized avocado contains 140 calories—or, to put it another way, a tablespoonful of purée contains 19 calories.

Unquestionably, it is among the most nourishing of all fruits and contains more protein than any other, over 2 per cent. The amount contained in half an average avocado is between 3 and 4 per cent of an adult's recommended daily protein requirement.

VITAMINS

The avocado is simply bursting with goodness—no wonder dieticians dream up avocado diets for people to enjoy. Vitamins A, B_1, B_2 and others from the B complex, C, E, K, HH and Folic acid are all present.

Vitamin A is essential for good vision in poor light and for healthy growth in children. Half an avocado contains almost 12 per cent of an adult's daily needs.

Thiamine (B_1), riboflavin (B_2) and pyridoxine (B_6) are found in avocados and play important roles in digestion and tissue metabolism. Half a pear contains the following percentages of the recommended daily requirements: betwen 5 and 8 per cent of thiamine, between 6 and 8 per cent of riboflavin and 9 per cent of pyridoxine.

Vitamin C, Ascorbic acid, is essential for a healthy skin and is believed to play a major role in the prevention and cure of the common cold. Half an avocado contains 15 per cent of an adult's daily needs.

Vitamin E is necessary for healthy child-bearing and lack of it leads to sterility in both men and women. Many beauty experts believe that this particular vitamin has special powers for keeping the skin and body youthful and sparkling with good health. Half an average avocado contains between 13 and 16 per cent of the recommended daily requirement for adults. The avocado can be used as an external beauty aid, too.

Vitamins K, HH and Folic acid are all necessary to healthy blood. Extra Folic acid is usually prescribed for pregnant women at ante-natal clinics. Half a pear contains 12 per cent of an adult's daily requirement.

MINERALS

Essential minerals to be found in the avocado pear include magnesium, copper, iron, calcium and potassium. These are all necessary to good health. Eat half a pear and you will be well on your way to meeting your daily requirements—12 to 14 per cent of magnesium, 7 to 13 per cent of iron, 4 per cent of phosphorous and 1 per cent of calcium. Other minerals are present, but in smaller quantities.

Finally, for those on a sodium-free diet, the sodium content is very low—only 10 mg in half an avocado.

In the Carribean, in the interior and mountainous areas where coconuts cannot thrive, avocados provide the chief dietary source of fat and oil.

In Central America, avocados often take the place of meat—they are appetising, nourishing, cheap and available throughout the year.

It was once calculated that 48 gallons of avocado oil could be extracted from an acre of avocado trees.

Buying Avocados

Like most tropical fruits, avocado pears are picked when they are mature but before they are ripe. Otherwise, they would be soggy and rotten before they became available in the shops. Often, they are still hard when they reach the shelves in the supermarket or at the greengrocer's. You can always buy unripe avocados and ripen them at home. Alternatively, see if the greengrocer has any ripe ones and these will often be reduced in price, especially at weekends, because they obviously cannot be kept for very much longer.

Testing For Ripeness

You cannot tell if an avocado pear is ripe simply by looking at it because the shades of colour differ from variety to variety. However, black spots on the skin are usually an indication that the avocado is, or soon will be, ready for eating.

Cradle the avocado gently in the palm of your hand. The ripe fruit will yield to very gentle pressure, rather like a ripe peach. Do not be tempted to squeeze the avocado or you will bruise the delicate flesh.

If you are still not sure if the fruit is ripe, pierce the stem end with a cocktail stick. If the stick slides in easily, then the avocado is ready for eating.

RIPENING AND STORING AVOCADOS

Do not be afraid to buy hard, unripe avocados. They will only take two or three days to ripen if they are left in a sunny place or in the airing cupboard. However, do not be tempted to ripen them on a radiator. They must be kept away from direct heat or they will become bitter tasting and totally inedible. Avocados ripen best at a temperature of between 60°F and 70°F (15.5°C—21°C). Leave them in the fruit bowl and they will be ready to eat in three to five days.

If you need to store ripe avocados, they can be kept in the refrigerator for up to a week without deteriorating. The temperature should not be lower than 42°F (5.5°C). If it falls below this, serious and irreparable damage is caused to the flesh. Halved avocados may be stored in the refrigerator. The exposed flesh should be sprinkled with lemon juice and covered with plastic wrap to prevent discoloration.

Whole avocados do not freeze successfully. The way round this is to scoop out the flesh and mash or purée it with a little lemon or lime juice and then put it in the freezer. Mousses, dips, ice-cream, soups and other prepared dishes using avocados can be deep frozen.

GETTING THE BEST FROM AVOCADOS

* Buy unripe avocados and store them in a warm place until they are ready for eating.

* Be adventurous and try out some new recipes —both savoury and sweet.

* Sprinkle exposed flesh with lemon or lime juice or cover with plastic wrap to prevent discoloration.

* Create your own *natural* beauty preparations.

* Chopped, sliced or mashed avocados go further than halves, especially if they are mixed with other ingredients.

* Take advantage of the delicate flavour and high nutritional content to tempt invalids and fussy eaters.

* Grow an ornamental houseplant from an avocado seed.

* Store ripe avocados in the refrigerator until you are ready to eat them.

* Firm avocados are ideal for serving in the shell; soft, ripe ones are perfect for purées.

AVOIDING DISAPPOINTMENT

* Never try to cook or eat unripe avocados.

* Handle them gently and do not be tempted to squeeze them when testing for ripeness.

* Do not expose avocados to direct heat.

* Do not combine avocados with strongly flavoured ingredients or you will lose their subtle taste.

* Do not leave flesh exposed to the air.

* Do not try to freeze whole avocados.

* Make sure that you never run out by keeping a supply of avocados ripening in a warm place.

* Use over-ripe avocados for homemade beauty treatments.

* Leaving the stone in the pulp helps to prevent discoloration—try it if you have to prepare a mixture in advance.

21

PREPARING AVOCADOS

Served in the shell, added to soups and salads, as a base for dips, mousses and creams, the avocado pear is both versatile and delicious. The cavity left when the seed or stone is removed could have been designed to hold a vinaigrette dressing or an exotic filling.

If you intend to serve an avocado in its shell, choose one that gives only slightly when cradled in the hand. Hass and Fuerte are excellent varieties; they are oval in shape, with firm skins and buttery flesh. Slice the avocado in half lengthways with a sharp stainless steel knife, cutting up to the stone and encircling the fruit. Gently rotate the two halves in opposite directions to separate them. Strike the stone with the sharp edge of the knife, and twist and lift the stone away. Discard the stone and sprinkle the avocado halves with lemon or lime juice to prevent discoloration. It is always sensible to prepare the fruit shortly before serving. Serve one half per person. Scoop out the flesh with an oval teaspoon.

Avocado vinaigrette is a classic starter. A little dressing is spooned into the cavity half an hour before serving. Other popular fillings include mayonnaise, either on its own or mixed with finely chopped, hard-boiled egg and chives; crab, prawns or shrimps; cream cheese mixed with chopped peppers, chopped cucumber or finely chopped onion; mixed citrus fruits and fruit salad. Yoghurt is a good base for fillings and can be mixed with peaches and apricots, orange segments or chopped tomatoes and cucumber. Some people like a piquant filling, to contrast with the smooth, rich avocado flesh. Others enjoy the subtle flavour and prefer their avocados plain, with perhaps a squeeze of lemon juice, salt and pepper and a garnish of chopped parsley or paprika.

Avocados lend themselves to experimentation and the creative cook can dream up dozens of different dishes with which to delight her family and friends. If you have a slightly riper avocado, then combine the flesh with other ingredients and pile it back into the shells, or simply serve the mixture on a lettuce leaf or in a grapefruit glass. Halve the pear and remove the stone. With a teaspoon, scoop the flesh from the shells, but be careful not to tear them if you intend to use the shells to hold the filling. Favourite mixtures include diced, crispy bacon, cream cheese and chopped, fresh chives, diced celery and chopped walnuts. Prepared in this manner, one avocado will serve three or four people.

You may wish to dice or slice an avocado, as an addition to a salad for example. Lightly score the skin with a sharp knife and carefully peel it off, starting at the narrow end. Halve the avocado and remove the stone. Be warned—the avocado will be as slippery as a bar of wet soap and must be handled with great care. Place it, flat side down, on a chopping board and cut it lengthways for long slices and crossways for half moons. Cut both ways to dice the flesh. Do not leave the flesh exposed for long or it will discolour. Sprinkle it with lemon juice and cover closely with plastic wrap.

AVOCADOS IN THE SHELL

For a perfect start to a meal, allow half an avocado per person and prepare one of these mouthwatering fillings. Halve the avocado, remove the stone, rub the flesh with lemon juice and add the filling of your choice. Garnish with chopped parsley, chives or a dusting of paprika, and serve.

To a couple of spoonfuls of *mayonnaise* add:

1. Chopped lobster and a couple of drops of chilli sauce.
2. Chopped chicken, chopped spring onions, sliced button mushrooms, salt, pepper and lemon juice.
3. An equal quantity of apple purée mixed with lemon juice and grated lemon rind.

To a couple of spoonfuls of *cream cheese* add:

1. Chopped green peppers and chopped onion.
2. Chopped cucumber or celery.

To a couple of spoonfuls of *cottage cheese* add:

1. Chopped spring onions, garlic, lemon juice and salt. Sprinkle paprika over the top and chill before serving.
2. Celery, apple and walnuts, all chopped up.

To a couple of spoonfuls of *sour cream* add:

1. Prawns, lemon juice, salt, pepper and chives. Dust the top with paprika and serve chilled.
2. Slivers of smoked salmon and lemon juice.

To a couple of spoonfuls of *yoghurt* add:

1. Chopped cucumber, lime juice, crushed garlic, salt and pepper.
2. Diced melon, chopped ginger, chopped mint, lemon juice, salt, pepper and a pinch of sugar.
3. Grapefruit and orange segments, grapes, lemon juice and mint leaves.

To a couple of spoonfuls of *white mustard sauce* add:

1. Flaked smoked mackerel.
2. Slivers of smoked salmon.

To a couple of spoonfuls of *vinaigrette* add:

1. Flaked tuna fish, chopped onion, chives and lemon juice.
2. Chopped tomato and onion, and freshly chopped parsley, basil and chives.

Avocado Hors d'oeuvres

Scrape the flesh from a fairly ripe avocado, mash it with a fork and add other ingredients to taste. Pile the mixture back into the shell or serve on a bed of lettuce leaves.

To mashed avocado add:

1. Cream cheese, lemon juice, grated onion, a few drops of Worcestershire sauce, Tabasco sauce and seasoning.
2. Minced chicken and mayonnaise.
3. Crabmeat, chopped onions, chopped celery, vinegar, lemon juice and salt. Top with mayonnaise mixed with a little tomato ketchup or purée.
4. Hard-boiled egg, chopped onion, thick cream, salt and pepper.
5. Cream cheese, tuna fish, parsley and lemon juice.
6. Chopped walnuts, celery, a little tomato purée and lemon juice and season with salt and pepper.
7. Many of the combinations suitable for fillings.

Chilled Avocado Soup

This soup is delicately flavoured and quite delicious. The green flesh near the skin of the avocados gives the soup its lovely colour.

1 tablespoon butter
1 onion, finely chopped
1-2 teaspoons curry powder
1¼ pints chicken stock

¼ pint dry white wine
3 avocado pears
salt
pinch sugar
dash Tabasco sauce
1 teaspoon lemon juice
½ pint double cream

Garnish:
1 lemon, finely sliced
3 tablespoons fresh parsley or chervil, chopped.

Melt the butter in a medium-sized saucepan and, gently fry the onion for 5-7 minutes, or until it is soft and translucent. Add the curry powder and cook, stirring constantly, for 5 minutes. Remove the pan from the heat.

Gradually stir in the chicken stock and wine. Return the pan to the heat and bring the liquid to the boil, stirring constantly, for 1 minute.

Peel and halve the avocados and discard the stones. Roughly chop the flesh and add it to the liquid. Add the salt, sugar, Tabasco sauce and lemon juice. Pour the mixture into an electric blender and blend to a fine purée. Alternatively, rub the mixture through a nylon strainer. Transfer the soup to a large bowl and chill in the refrigerator for 1 hour.

Lightly beat the cream to thicken it slightly and fold it into the soup. Check the seasoning and pour the soup into a tureen or individual soup bowls. Garnish with lemon slices and sprinkle over the chopped parsley. Serve immediately.

Serves 6

CHICKEN AND AVOCADO CASSEROLE

Chicken and avocado combine remarkably well. The avocado topping makes this chicken dish rather special.

3 tablespoons plain flour
salt and pepper
1 teaspoon dried basil
grated rind of 1 lemon
4 chicken pieces
3 oz butter
1 onion, chopped
½ pint chicken stock
¼ pint dry white wine
1 avocado pear
1 teaspoon lemon juice
¼ pint double cream
2 teaspoons olive oil

Preheat the oven to 190°C (375°F), gas mark 5.

Mix together 2 tablespoons of flour, salt, pepper, basil and lemon rind. Coat the chicken pieces in the seasoned flour.

Melt 2 oz of the butter in a large frying pan and fry the chicken pieces for 8-10 minutes, or until they are well browned on all sides. With a slotted spoon, transfer them to an ovenproof casserole.

Add the remaining butter to the pan. Gently fry the onion for 5-7 minutes, or until it is soft and translucent. Sprinkle over the remaining tablespoon of flour and cook, stirring constantly, for 1 minute.

Remove the pan from the heat and gradually stir in the stock and the wine. Bring to the boil, stirring constantly, and pour over the chicken pieces. Cover and cook for 1 hour, or until the chicken is tender and cooked through.

Peel and halve the avocado and discard the stone. Cut the halves lengthways into ¼-inch slices. Sprinkle over the lemon juice.

Remove the casserole from the oven. Uncover and set aside until the cooking juices stop bubbling. Then stir in the cream. Arrange the avocado slices on top and carefully brush them with oil.

Return the casserole, covered, to the oven and cook for a further 10 minutes. Serve immediately.

Serves 4

AVOCADO SAUCE

A delicious pale green sauce to serve with cold salmon or smoked mackerel.

1 ripe avocado pear
5 fl oz sour cream
1 tablespoon lemon juice
salt and black pepper
1 tablespoon chopped chives

Peel and halve the avocado and discard the stone. Mash the flesh with a fork.

Blend in the sour cream, lemon juice and salt and pepper until thoroughly combined. Sprinkle the sauce with chopped chives.

AVOCADO MOUSSE

This mousse has a refreshing sharp flavour.

¼ pint hot chicken stock
½ oz gelatine
2 ripe avocado pears
1 tablespoon lemon juice
1 clove of garlic, crushed (optional)
salt and black pepper
½ pint mayonnaise
¼ pint double cream, lightly whipped

Garnish:
cucumber slices
prawns

Dissolve the gelatine in the chicken stock.

Peel and halve the avocados and discard the stones. Roughly chop the flesh.

Put the avocado flesh and the lemon juice in an electric blender and blend to a fine purée. Alternatively, push the avocado flesh through a nylon strainer and then beat in the lemon juice.

Stir in the stock, garlic and plenty of salt and pepper. Allow to cool.

When cold, fold in the mayonnaise and cream. Pour into a lightly oiled 2-pint mould and chill, tightly covered with plastic wrap, in the refrigerator until set.

Not more than 30 minutes before serving, turn out the mousse on to a flat dish. Decorate with cucumber slices and prawns.

Serves 6

TOMATO SALAD WITH AVOCADO DRESSING

Avocado mayonnaise goes perfectly with chicken, tuna fish and egg salads.

1 lettuce, washed and shaken dry
1 lb tomatoes
1 tablespoon chopped chives

Avocado dressing:
1 avocado pear
5 tablespoons mayonnaise
1 tablespoon grated onion
1 tablespoon lemon juice
dash Worcestershire sauce
salt and pepper

First make the dressing. Peel and halve the avocado and discard the stone. Roughly chop the flesh.

Put the avocado flesh, mayonnaise, grated onion and lemon juice in an electric blender and blend to a smooth purée. Alternatively, rub the avocado through a nylon strainer and then beat in the mayonnaise, onion and lemon juice until thoroughly combined.

Stir in the Worcestershire sauce, salt and pepper to taste. Set aside.

Separate the lettuce leaves and arrange them on a serving platter. Thinly slice the tomatoes and arrange them on top of the lettuce. Spoon over the avocado dressing. Sprinkle with chopped chives and serve immediately.

Serves 4

Avocado And Orange Salad

Add sliced grapefruit and finely chopped green pepper for an interesting variation.

½ lettuce, washed and shaken dry
2 oranges, peeled and sliced
1 Spanish onion, peeled and thinly sliced
1 avocado pear

Dressing:
3 tablespoons olive oil
1 tablespoon white wine vinegar
1 tablespoon orange juice
1 teaspoon dried marjoram
1 teaspoon French mustard
salt and pepper

First make the dressing. Combine the ingredients in a screw-top jar and shake well. Set aside.

Separate the lettuce leaves and arrange them on a serving platter. Arrange the orange and onion slices alternately over the top in overlapping rings. Set aside.

Peel and halve the avocado and discard the stone. Dice the flesh and pile it into the centre of the serving dish. Pour over the dressing and serve immediately.

Serves 2

In Jamaica, avocados are served with a dressing of rum and fresh lime juice.

AVOCADO CREAM

This unusual dessert is wonderfully light and fluffy—and very easy to make. It is especially good served with fresh fruit salad.

2 avocado pears
4 tablespoons caster sugar
juice of 1 lemon
8 fl oz double cream, stiffly whipped

Peel and halve the avocados and discard the stones. Roughly chop the flesh.

Put the avocado flesh, sugar and lemon juice in an electric blender and blend to a smooth purée. Alternatively, rub the flesh through a nylon strainer and then beat in the sugar and lemon juice until thoroughly combined.

Fold in the cream, using a metal spoon. Transfer the mixture to individual serving dishes and chill in the refrigerator for 1 hour.

Serve with langue du chat biscuits.

Serves 4

AVOCADO ICE-CREAM

Top with pistachio nuts or toasted almonds.

1 large avocado pear
2 tablespoons orange or lime juice
2 eggs, separated
2 oz caster sugar
½ pint double cream

Peel and halve the avocados and discard the stones. Roughly chop the flesh.

Put the avocado flesh, orange juice and egg yolks in an electric blender and blend to a fine purée. Alternatively, push the avocado flesh through a nylon strainer and then beat in the fruit juice and egg yolks until thoroughly combined.

Beat the egg whites until stiff. Whisk in the sugar, a teaspoonful at a time.

Whip the cream until it forms peaks and fold it into the meringue mixture. Fold in the avocado purée.

Pour the ice-cream mixture into a freezer tray, cover and freeze for several hours.

Serves 4

In Brazil, the avocado is more of a dessert than a staple food—it is made into delicious ice-cream.

GUACAMOLE

This very popular dip originated in Mexico and there are many variations. It makes a delicious filling for stuffed tomatoes, too.

3 avocado pears
3 teaspoons lemon juice
2 teaspoons olive oil
salt and pepper
1 clove garlic, crushed (optional)
½ teaspoon ground coriander
1 hard-boiled egg, finely chopped
1 small green pepper, seeded and chopped
1-2 green chillis, blanched and chopped
2 spring onions, chopped
1 tomato, peeled, seeded and chopped

Peel and halve the avocados and discard the stones. Roughly chop the flesh. Mash the flesh to a pulp with a fork.

Beat in the lemon juice, olive oil, salt and pepper, garlic, coriander, egg, green pepper, chillis to taste, spring onions and tomato.

Serve immediately or cover with plastic wrap and store in the refrigerator for 1-2 hours.

Serve with sliced, raw vegetables, spring onions, crisps, pretzels and savoury biscuits.

Makes 12 fl oz

OTHER TIMES TO EAT AVOCADOS

For a quick and nourishing snack—spread mashed avocado on toast and season with salt and black pepper.

For an easy breakfast—poach an egg in butter and serve in the cavity of half an avocado pear.

For a sustaining open sandwich—arrange crisp, cooked bacon and slices of avocado in alternate layers on a slice of French bread. Top with 1 oz grated Cheddar cheese and grill until the cheese has melted.

For a hangover cure—mix together half an avocado pear puréed, 1 teaspoon honey and 1 orange, peeled and chopped.

To brighten up a miserable day—make this avocado mixture and serve with toast triangles and chilled champagne. Mix together one puréed avocado, 1 tablespoon of mayonnaise, 1 crushed garlic clove, salt, pepper, 1 teaspoon French mustard, 2 teaspoons lemon juice and a dash of chilli sauce.

For a lunchtime treat—bake four potatoes, scoop out the flesh and mash with an avocado pear, finely chopped spring onion and salt and pepper. Pile the mixture back into the shells. Sprinkle over 4 tablespoons of grated Cheddar cheese and grill until it has melted.

For a summer picnic—hard-boil six eggs and allow them to cool. Shell and halve the eggs and carefully remove the yolks. Mash the yolks with half an avocado pear and 1 teaspoon grated onion. Spoon the mixture back into the whites and season with a little cayenne pepper.

Add a sparkle to unexciting salads—add half an avocado pear, diced.

Serve sophisticated hamburgers—top them with 2 tablespoons of guacamole.

For a special occasion—serve avocado with grilled steaks instead of maitre d'hotel butter. Mash the flesh of an avocado pear with chopped parsley, lemon juice and salt and pepper and chill.

Cook the Mexican way—add avocados to stuffings for turkey, chicken, red peppers and tomatoes.

Four or five tortillas, an avocado and a cup of coffee make a good meal, say the Indians of Guatemala.

AVOCADOS AND BEAUTY

The secrets of the avocado pear as a beauty aid were discovered long ago by the Aztec, Inca and Mayan women, who used the oil to protect their skins against the dry winds of Central America.

The combination of rich oils and vitamin E is excellent for keeping the skin soft and youthful and the hair healthy and shining. Many beauticians think of vitamin E as the 'youth vitamin' and avocado cosmetics are a natural way of helping to prevent and of treating those insidious signs of the years—wrinkles, crepey neck and sagging and flabby muscles.

Since the 1930s, avocado oil has been sold to the cosmetics trade and used in beauty creams and massage oils. Its high degree of penetration is comparable to that of lanolin and it is far kinder to the skin than mineral, animal and other vegetable oils.

Beauty creams and treatments made with ripe avocados are quick and easy to prepare at home. Only if you use natural ingredients which you mix yourself can you know for certain what goes into your beauty preparations. Avocado beauty is natural beauty—very much the hallmark of the 1980s look. Another important consideration, again very much in tune with the times, is the fact that natural, homemade beauty products make economic sense. It is very satisfying to know that you are not paying high prices for expensive packaging or for a famous brand name.

Give your face and hair a treat. Summer weather and holidays can play havoc with the complexion, and the combination of sun, sand, sea and wind spells disaster for the hair. Avocado preparations are ideal for restoring the balance and repairing the damage.

Many women have delicate and sensitive skins and find commercial products irritating. For them, avocado creams, with their penetrating natural oils, prove invaluable.

Avocados which are too ripe to eat need not be wasted. They are ideal for preparing beauty aids. Use ripe, soft fruits and prepare the treatments as near to the time you wish to use them as possible. They can be stored for up to 48 hours in the refrigerator, covered with plastic wrap.

Most of the following preparations require only half a pear. If you haven't already done so, why not eat the other half to provide *inner* beauty and take advantage of all those vitamins and minerals. It has only 140 calories, after all.

CLEANSING CREAM

Ingredients: ½ avocado pear
1 egg yolk, lightly beaten
8 fl oz plain yoghurt

To mix: Scoop the avocado flesh out of the shell and mash it to a smooth pulp. Gradually beat in the egg yolk and stir in the yoghurt.

To use: Gently massage the cream into the face, working from the centre outwards. Finally massage around the jaw and neck. Wipe off with cotton wool.

COMPLEXION TREATMENT
(Oily skin)

Ingredients: ½ avocado pear
1 egg white
1 teaspoon lemon juice

To mix: Scoop the avocado flesh out of the shell and mash it to a smooth pulp. Beat in the egg white and lemon juice to form a smooth paste.

To use: Thoroughly cleanse the face and neck. Apply the mask with the fingertips, paying special attention to oily areas, such as the nose, cheekbones and chin. Leave for 20 minutes and then remove with cotton wool and lukewarm water. Pat dry.

COMPLEXION TREATMENT
(Dry skin)

Ingredients: ½ avocado pear
1 egg yolk, well beaten
1 teaspoon rose water

To mix: Scoop the avocado flesh out of the shell and mash it to a smooth pulp. Gradually beat the egg yolk and rose water to form a smooth paste.

To use: Thoroughly cleanse the face and neck. Apply the mask with the fingertips, paying special attention to dry areas, such as the forehead, under the eyes and the neck. Leave for 20 minutes and then remove with cotton wool and lukewarm water. Pat dry.

NIGHT OIL TREATMENT

Reserve an avocado shell after preparing one of the above treatments, or after eating half a pear. Make sure that all the flesh has been scraped off.

Turn the shell inside out and rub it over the face and neck, after they have been thoroughly cleansed. Leave overnight. Next morning, wash the face and neck in lukewarm water and pat dry.

HOLIDAY CARE SKIN TONER

Ingredients: ½ avocado pear
               1 teaspoon clear honey
               1 teaspoon single cream

To mix: Scoop the avocado flesh out of the
               shell and mash it to a smooth pulp.
               Beat in the honey and cream until all
               the ingredients are thoroughly
               combined.

To use: Thoroughly cleanse the face and neck.
               Apply the mask with the fingertips,
               paying special attention to 'danger'
               areas, such as the nose and
               cheekbones. Leave for 20 minutes and
               then remove with cotton wool and
               lukewarm water. Pat dry.

LUXURY TREATMENT FOR ELBOWS, HEELS AND KNEES

Reserve an avocado shell after preparing one of the
above treatments, or after eating half a pear. Make
sure that all the flesh has been scraped off.

Turn the shell inside out and rub it vigorously over
the elbows, heels and knees to remove dry skin and
soften rough patches.

'DE-BAG' EYE TREATMENT

Peel an avocado pear and cut it in half, discarding the stone. Reserve one half for one of the above treatments or for eating. Take the other half and cut it lengthways into ¼-inch slices.

Lie down flat and place two or three slices under each eye. Leave for 20 minutes.

CONDITIONING SHAMPOO FOR HOLIDAY HAIR

Ingredients:	½ avocado pear 4 fl oz baby shampoo 4 fl oz warm water
To mix:	Scoop the avocado flesh out of the shell and mash it to a smooth pulp. Stir in the shampoo and warm water until all the ingredients are thoroughly blended.
To use:	Wet the hair thoroughly with warm water. Rub in half the avocado shampoo, massaging it well into the scalp. Rinse thoroughly with warm water. Rub in the remaining shampoo. Leave for 5 minutes and then rinse thoroughly with warm water. If any traces of stickiness remain, shampoo again with a very small quantity of baby shampoo and rinse thoroughly.

Avocado Manicure

Ingredients:
½ avocado pear
1 egg yolk, lightly beaten
1 teaspoon single cream

To mix:
Scoop the avocado flesh out of the shell and mash it to a smooth pulp. Reserve the shell. Beat the egg yolk and cream into the pulp until all the ingredients are thoroughly combined.

To use:
Rub the mixture well into the hands, paying special attention to the fingertips, nails and cuticles. Leave for 15 minutes. Gently ease back the cuticles with a cotton wool bud or manicurist's orange stick. Wash the hands in lukewarm water.

Then turn the avocado shell inside out and rub it over the hands, paying special attention to dry areas, such as the palms and between the fingers. Leave overnight and wash off in lukewarm water in the morning.

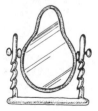

FOLKLORE

Almost every edible fruit and vegetable (and some inedible ones too) has, at some time, been claimed as an aphrodisiac. The avocado's reputation in this respect is as dubious and spurious as the tomato's or the pomegranate's. However, before dismissing the passionate possibilities completely, remember that the avocado is a very sensuous fruit. Its creamy texture, subtle flavour, delicate scent, exquisite colour and sophisticated reputation make it eminently suitable for romantic candlelit *dîners à deux*. After that, it is up to you.

The avocado has also been credited with powers of rejuvenation. The suggestion is, 'an avocado a day keeps the years at bay'. Sadly, no magical formula to turn back the clock has yet been discovered. There is, however, a small element of truth in this idea because the avocado can be used as a natural beauty aid and is particularly efficacious in treating the signs of the relentlessly passing years—crepey neck, wrinkles and dry and aging skin. Also, it is such a nutritious fruit that regular inclusion in the diet helps to keep you fit and well and, therefore, young and beautiful.

Powers of oratory and skilful persuasion have also been attributed to the fruit. So perhaps you should make sure that you eat an avocado pear before going to see the bank manager. Undoubtedly, the rich oils in the flesh help to lubricate the throat but the idea that the avocado bestows fluency probably arose from the confusion of names. The original Aztec name,

Ahuacatl, was corrupted by the Spanish to *avocado,* meaning advocate, a person who pleads in courts of justice.

Myths associated with childbirth are many and occur in almost every country in the world. Eating avocado pears is certainly no hardship, although whether it will ensure an easy birth is not so certain. However, it is a delicious way of obtaining many necessary vitamins and minerals during pregnancy and is an especially palatable form of iron. Also, the presence of vitamin E, essential to healthy child-bearing, does add a little weight to this superstition.

Equally, carving the avocado seed into the shape of a boy or girl is unlikely to have any effect on the sex of the unborn child, but it is a charming custom. This idea may have been prompted by the way the seed nestles so safely and securely in the womb-like pear.

AVOCADOS, HEALTH AND MEDICINE

The benefits of the avocado pear are many and its valuable vitamins and minerals, combined with its delicious flavour, make it a useful contribution to the well-balanced diet. However, it has advantages in addition to its helpfulness in maintaining normal good health.

One of the most interesting and important factors from the point of view of health is that the avocado pear contains no cholesterol. Cholesterol is a contentious subject in medical discussions. It can play a role in causing and aggravating some serious conditions, but whether the cholesterol is related to dietary intake is debatable. In arteriosclerosis, hardening of the arteries, cholesterol is deposited on artery walls, narrowing the passage. The heart has, therefore to work harder to push the blood along. This may be a contributory factor to heart conditions and can cause raised blood pressure.

Cholesterol may also play a causative part in gallstone disease. Research shows that susceptibility to gallstones seems to be increased in people whose diets are high in cholesterol and low in fibre.

Avocado pears are excellent for people on low sodium diets followed, for example, by those with certain metabolic disorders, high blood pressure and some kidney conditions. Half an average-sized avocado contains 10.0 mg of sodium.

The carbohydrate content is also very low. Half an avocado contains about 3.8 grams of carbohydrate. This is not only good for slimmers on a low-carbohydrate diet, but also makes it a useful food for diabetics.

The avocado has been shown to have skin healing properties. If it is combined with the right medicinal substances, it can make effective skin unguents and ointments.

Avocados are a good way to introduce babies to solid foods. They are easy to eat and easy to digest. They are soft enough for a baby to eat raw, and therefore none of the vitamins is destroyed by cooking. Also, most babies dislike strong flavours, so the delicate tasting avocado scores with both mother and child.

AVOCADOS AND THE SLIMMER

It so often happens that the foods which taste the most delicious are the very ones banned by a strict slimming regime. Avocados are the happy exception to this and can prove the basis for a wide selection of slimming dishes. Whatever type of diet you are following, except perhaps a low fat diet, the avocado is suitable for inclusion.

The most popular way to slim is to cut down on the number of calories eaten. The good news for these slimmers is that one tablespoon of avocado purée contains only 19 calories. Half an average-sized avocado contains about 140 calories.

Cutting out carbohydrates, starches and sugars, is another popular and effective way to lose weight. And once again, the avocado scores. Half an avocado contains only 3.8 grams of carbohydrate. That is, about 4.7 per cent of the fruit comprises carbohydrate, which is perfect for a low-carbohydrate diet.

Both high fat and high protein diets are becoming increasingly popular because they extend the range of 'permitted' foods, while encouraging the body to use up its stores of fat. The avocado is rich in both of these and ideally suited for inclusion in such diets.

Many slimmers worry that by drastically altering their eating patterns they may be depriving themselves of vitamins and minerals. What fruit could be more nutritious than the avocado pear? Include it in your diet and you are well on the way to getting your daily requirement.

A good tip for would-be slimmers who have a tendency to raid the biscuit tin whenever they feel a hunger pang or the need for a nibble, is to keep a supply of avocados handy. Cut a generous slice, sprinkle it lightly with salt and eat it in your fingers to combat that terrible empty feeling. Total calories are about 35, as opposed to nearer 150 if you eat just one ounce of biscuits. Avocados are also delicious served as a first course with a low-calorie dressing or mayonnaise.

You certainly do not have to be on a diet to enjoy the recipes that follow.

SLIMMERS' SOUP

This soup is equally good served chilled with chopped spring onions sprinkled over the top.

2 ripe avocado pears
1 pint chicken stock
5 fl oz plain yoghurt
salt and pepper
juice of 1 lemon
2 tablespoons parsley, finely chopped

Peel and halve the avocados and discard the stones. Roughly chop the flesh.

Put the avocado flesh and the chicken stock in an electric blender and blend to a fine purée. Alternatively, push the avocado flesh through a nylon strainer and then beat in the chicken stock until thoroughly combined.

Pour the mixture into a medium-sized saucepan and slowly bring to the boil. Season with salt and pepper and simmer very gently for 10 minutes.

Remove from the heat and stir in the yoghurt, lemon juice and most of the chopped parsley. Heat through but do not allow to boil. Check the seasoning and serve immediately, garnished with the remaining parsley.

Serves 4
185 calories per serving

AVOCADO WITH HAM

This colourful dish makes an excellent and eye-catching first course. Serve with brown bread and butter if your diet will allow.

6 thin slices Parma ham
1 teaspoon French mustard
1 avocado pear
1 teaspoon lemon juice
6 lettuce leaves, washed and shaken dry

Spread the ham with the mustard and cut it into strips about ¾ inch wide.

Peel and halve the avocado and discard the stone. Cut the halves lengthways into ¼-inch slices. Sprinkle over the lemon juice.

Arrange the lettuce leaves on a serving platter. Arrange the ham strips and avocado slices alternately over the top and serve immediately.

Serves 3
180 calories per serving

SPEEDY AVOCADO LUNCH

A tasty and nutritious slimming meal.

4 oz cottage cheese
1 green pepper, seeded and chopped
4 celery stalks, chopped
1 dessert apple, peeled, cored and diced
salt and pepper
2 avocado pears
1 tablespoon lemon juice
½ lettuce, washed and shaken dry

Mix together the cottage cheese, green pepper, celery and apple. Season to taste and set aside.

Halve the avocados and discard the stones. Peel off the skins and brush the flesh all over with the lemon juice. Pile the cheese mixture into the cavities and chill in the refrigerator for 30 minutes.

Separate the lettuce leaves and divide them between four serving plates. Place one avocado half on each plate and serve immediately.

Serves 4
210 calories per serving

In the West Indies, avocados are eaten as a vegetable, with no seasoning but salt.

AVOCADO DESSERT

Prepare the orange, grapes and pear in advance. They will make their own juice.

1 banana, peeled and sliced
1 orange, peeled and separated into segments
4 oz grapes, peeled and halved
1 pear, peeled, cored and diced
2-3 teaspoons calorie-free sweetener (optional)
2 avocado pears
2 teaspoons lemon juice

Combine the banana, orange, grapes and pear in a shallow dish. Sprinkle over sweetener to taste. Chill in the refrigerator for 30 minutes.

Halve the avocados and discard the stones. Sprinkle the lemon juice over the cut sides. Pile the fruit mixture into the cavities and spoon over the juice. Serve immediately.

Serves 4
190 calories per serving

AVOCADO LEMON JELLY

For a more substantial, but not so slimming, dessert, add a little lemon juice and a couple of tablespoons of single cream to the jelly along with the avocado purée.

1 avocado pear
1 lemon jelly, made with 1 pint water and cooled to setting point
orange segments

Peel and halve the avocado and discard the stone. Roughly chop the flesh.

Purée the flesh in an electric blender. Alternatively, rub it through a nylon strainer.

Gradually beat the avocado purée into the lemon jelly until they are thoroughly combined. Transfer to a mould and chill in the refrigerator for 1 hour, or until completely set. Decorate with orange segments.

Serves 6
80 calories per serving

How To Grow An Avocado Tree

Do not automatically throw out the avocado seed with the rubbish. Avocados make attractive, unusual and interesting houseplants. They are fairly easy to grow in a pot and usually reach a height of between 2 and 3 feet. They may grow taller and at least one 10-foot specimen has been recorded.

Unfortunately for all avocado lovers, pot-grown avocados will not bear fruit, however large they grow. Even transferring them to a heated greenhouse will not do the trick, as it is necessary to graft on a mature scion, or young shoot.

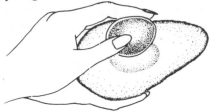

First of all, carefully remove the large seed from the centre of an avocado pear. Wash it in lukewarm water to remove all traces of fruit pulp. Cut off the pointed tip, using a sharp knife. Insert four tooth-picks or matchsticks about half an inch deep into the seed about one-third of the way down. Space these evenly around the seed and make sure that they are firm enough to support its weight.

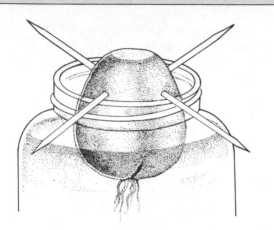

Fill a narrow, glass jar with distilled water and lower the seed into it so that the sticks rest on the rim. The top of the seed should stick out above the water and the bottom half inch should be submerged.

Set the jar in a warm place, but not in direct sunlight. Add more distilled water when necessary to keep the bottom of the seed submerged.

Within two to six weeks, the seed will start to split apart. Curly white roots will begin to grow downwards into the water. Next, a stem will begin to grow upwards. This may be either reddish-coloured or green, and sometimes double stems grow.

It can take as long as eight weeks for the avocado seed to split and show signs of life. If nothing has happened by then, abandon that seed and try another. You may have started with an immature seed which will never grow.

When the stem has grown 6 inches tall, cut it off halfway down, using a sharp knife. This will encourage branches to grow and create a bushier plant.

When several leaves have developed and the roots are thick, the avocado plant is ready for potting.

Pot the avocado plant in a 4-inch earthenware pot. Put in a good layer of crocks to allow free drainage and fill the pot to within half an inch of the rim with rich compost. Make a hollow in the centre of the compost, large enough to take the seed and the roots growing from it without damaging them.

Carefully remove the plant from the water and remove the toothpicks or matchsticks which have been supporting the seed. Place the seed and roots in the prepared hollow, taking care not to bend or break them. Gently sprinkle compost over the roots and seed but do not firm. Water the plant in.

Place the plant in a warm, light position but not in direct sunlight. Keep it well away from draughts. Water when the compost feels dry below the surface, but not too frequently. Do not leave the plant standing in water for prolonged periods. During the growing season, feed it weekly with a commercial indoor plant fertilizer, following the manufacturer's instructions. Spray the leaves occasionally with a fine mist of tepid water. From time to time, pinch back the branches at the tips to encourage leafy growth.

Pot on the avocado plant before the roots become pot-bound, but no more frequently than once a year. Provide a small supporting stake, once the plant reaches a height of about 10 inches.

ACKNOWLEDGEMENTS

Marina Andrews of Town and Country Beauty
    Salons
Australian High Commission, London
Calavo Growers of California
Carmel Produce of Israel
Embassy of Israel, London
Embassy of Mexico, London
Shankman Laboratories, Los Angeles
South African Embassy, London
United States Agricultural Trade Office, London
University of California

If you would like further information on all the titles in this series, and on other Piatkus gift books, please send a stamped addressed envelope to

Judy Piatkus (Publishers) Limited
17 Brook Road,
Loughton, Essex